COTY

The Clean-up Mission

Coty's Adventures

Vol.2

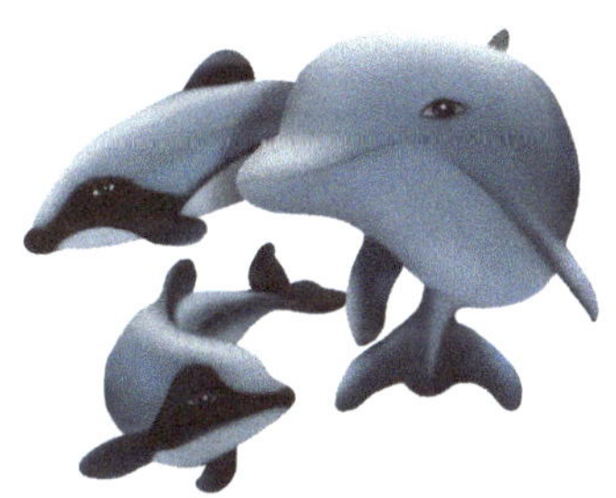

by: Tejveer Rathore

Illustrated by: Joseline Ca

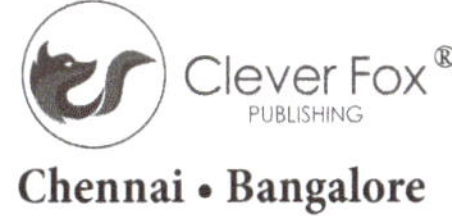

Clever Fox®
PUBLISHING

Chennai • Bangalore

FOX PUBLISHING
ndia

by CLEVER FOX PUBLISHING 2024
© Tejveer Rathore 2024

Reserved.
-93-56487-18-5

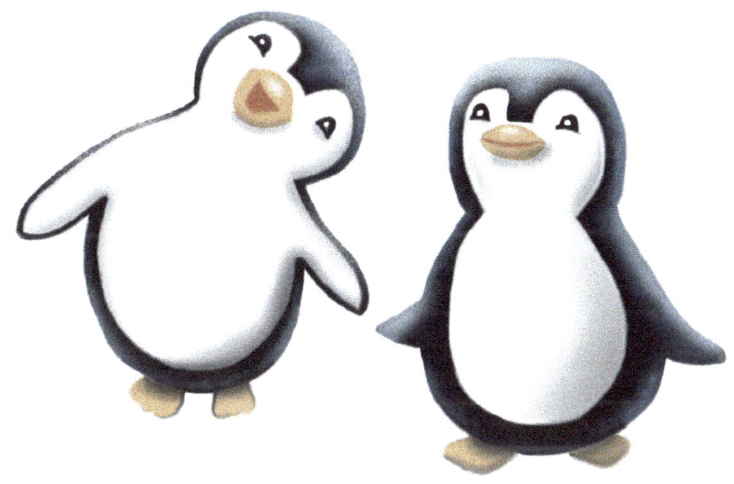

Dedication

"To all animal lovers and children of the world,
especially the child we all carry within."

T&J

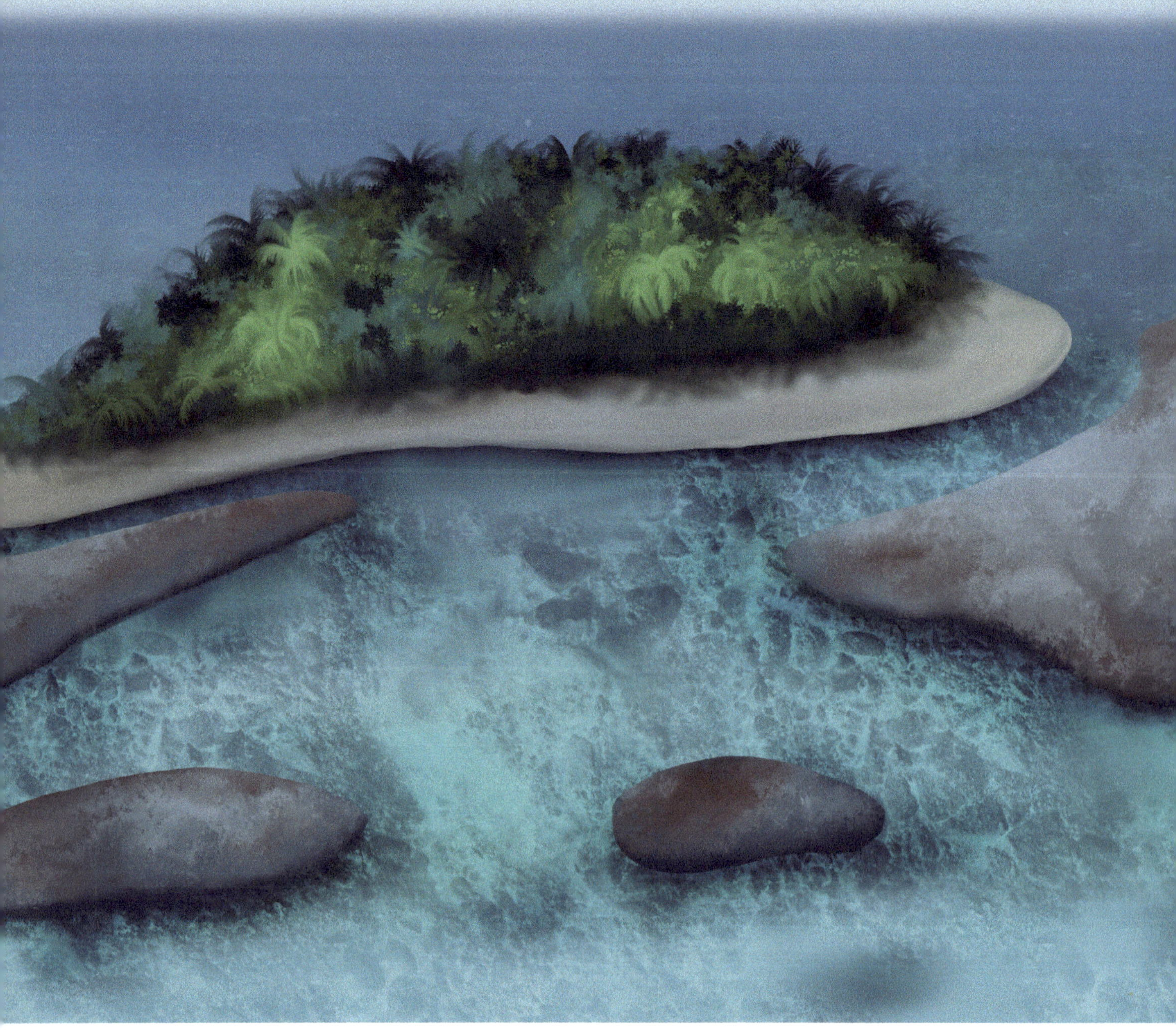

t's almost winter on Nanao Island. The sea is beginning to feel slightly colc

Coty's mother has a plan to escape the cold winter.
"We will be travelling to Kiwiland, in the south where it's warmer,
to visit our cousins, the Maui dolphins."

Coty has never been more excited but has a question
on her mind, "Mother, how will we find our way to Kiwiland
through the deep, dark ocean?"

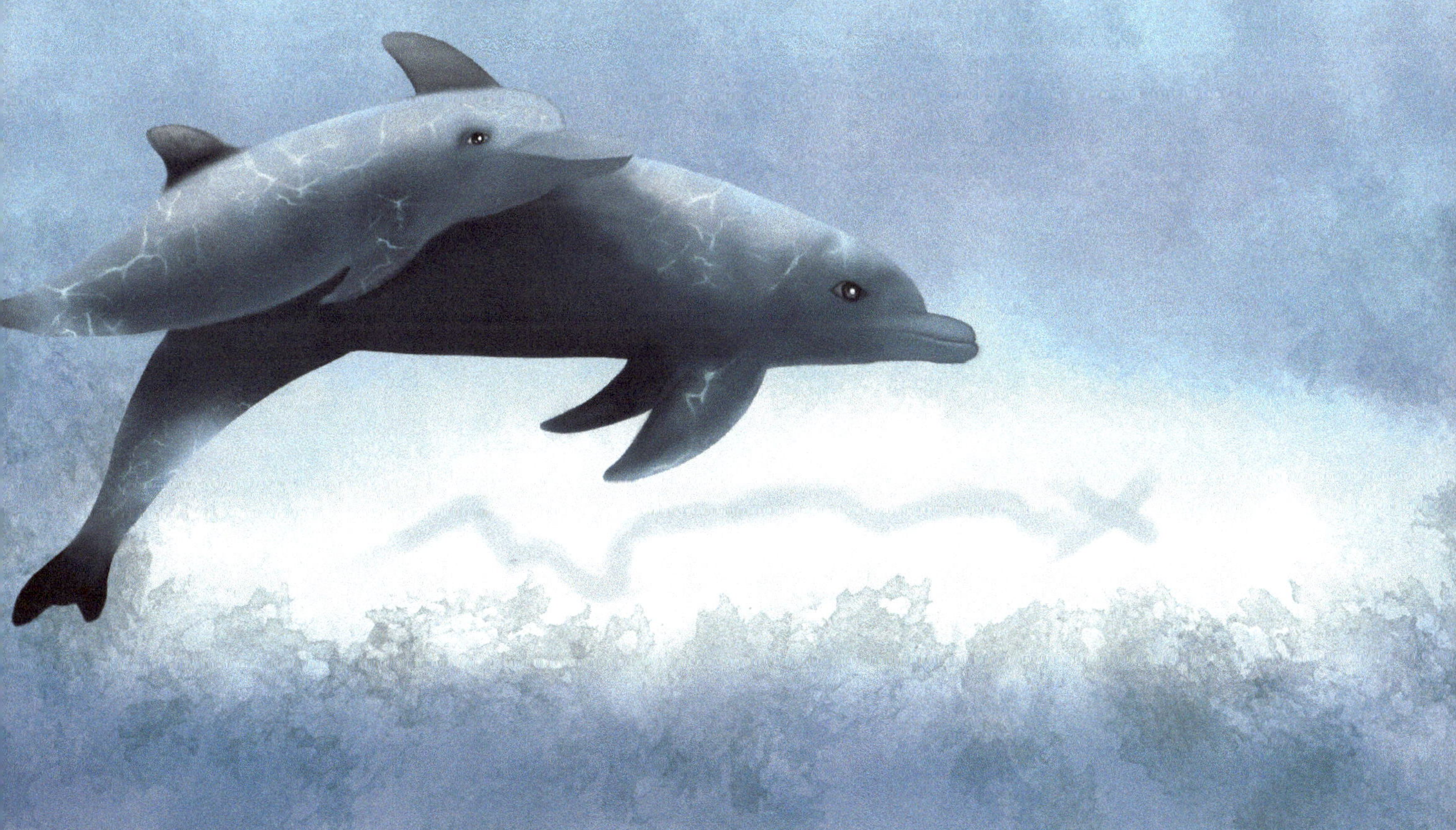

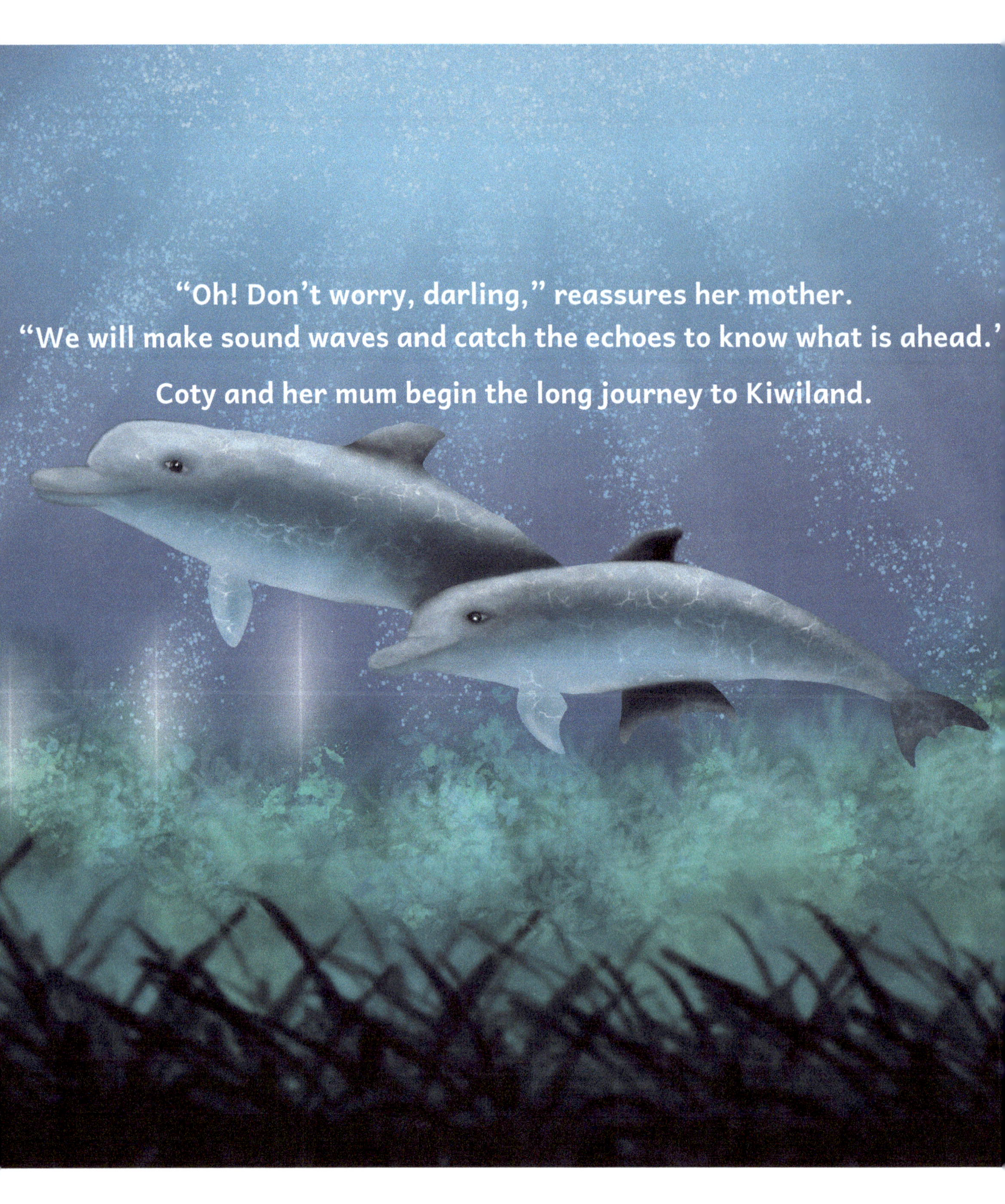

"Oh! Don't worry, darling," reassures her mother.
"We will make sound waves and catch the echoes to know what is ahead."
Coty and her mum begin the long journey to Kiwiland.

Along the way they come across a humpback whale.
Unlike the other humpback whales known to Coty, this one has
deep marks on her back and fins.

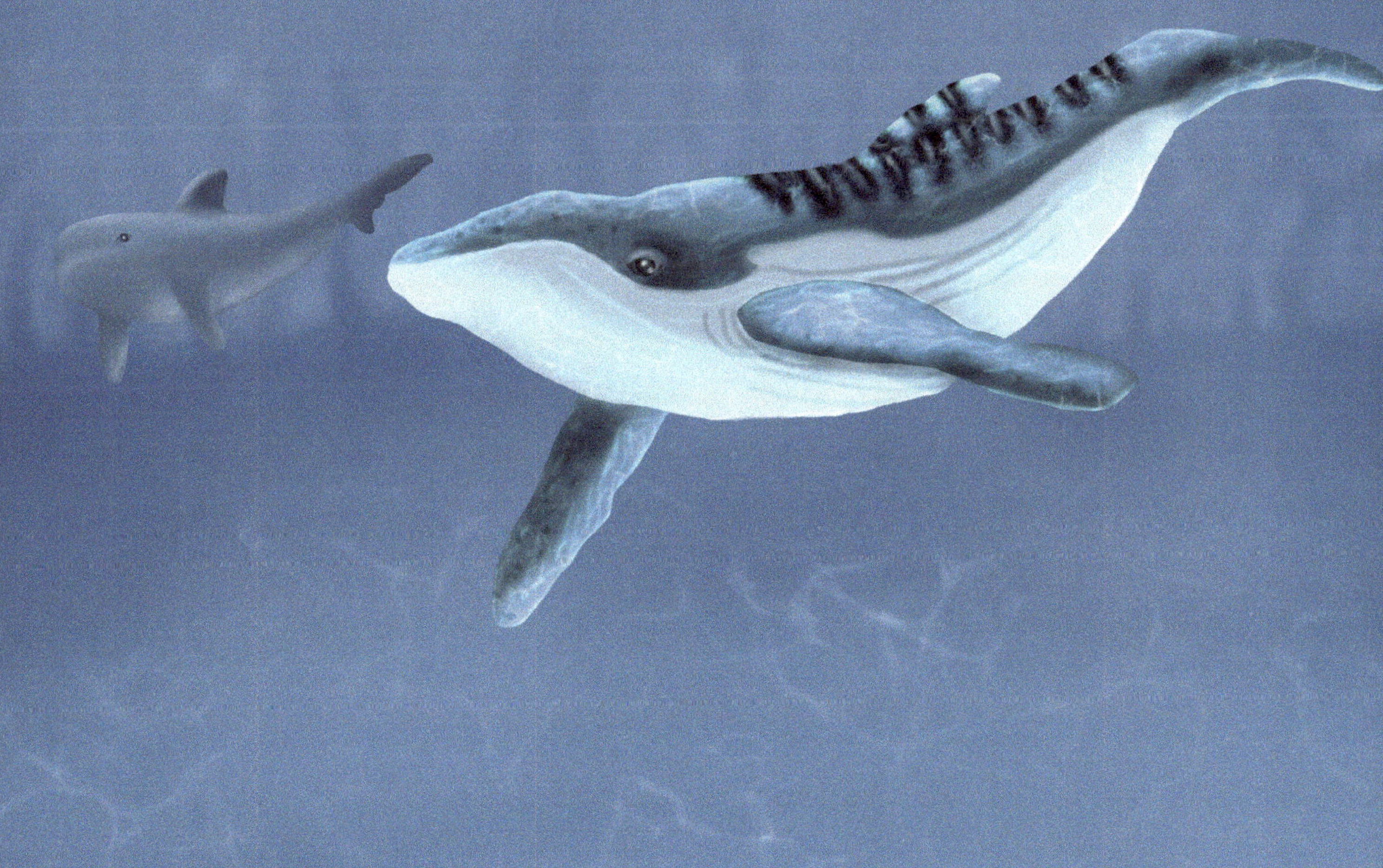

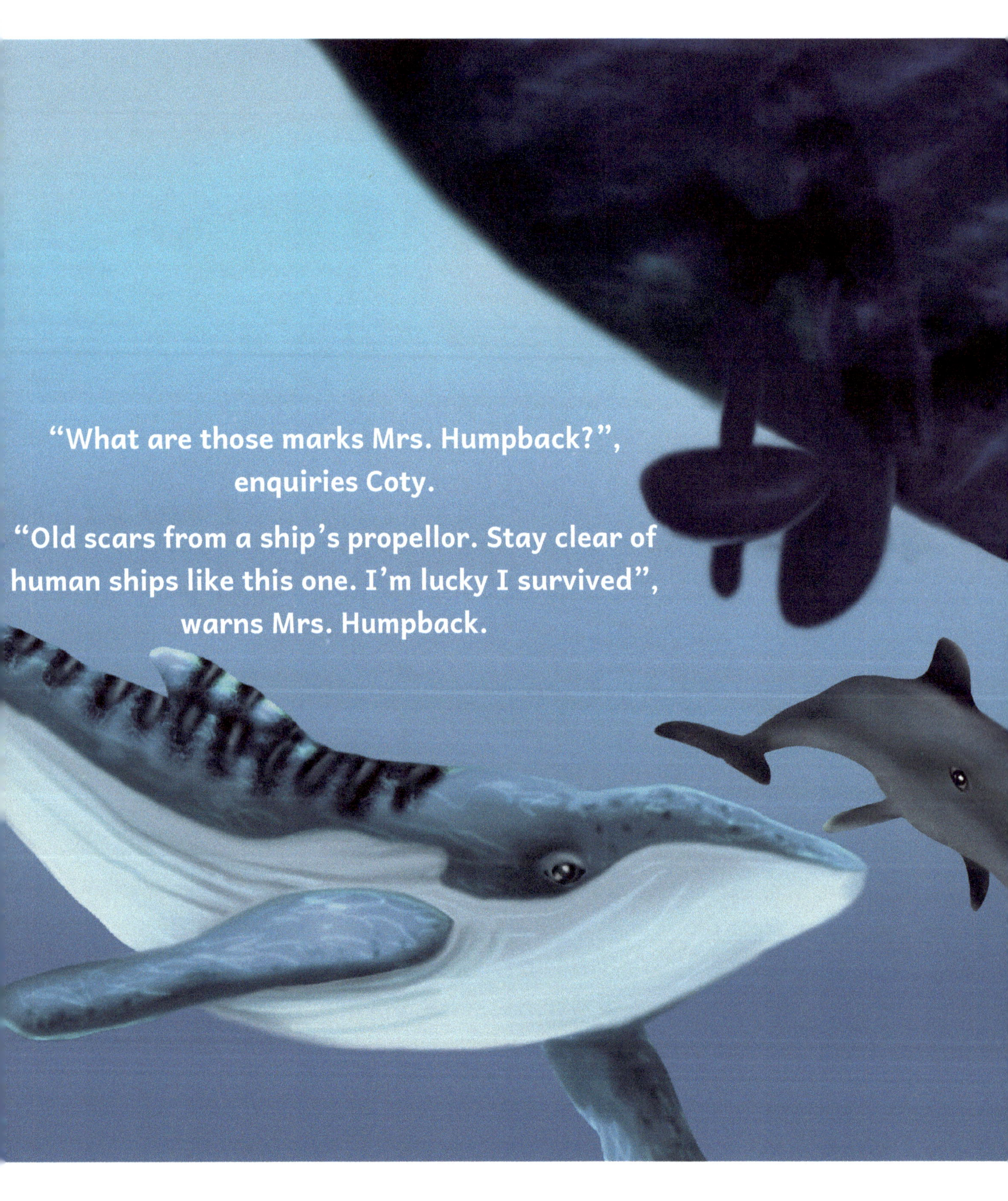
"What are those marks Mrs. Humpback?",
enquiries Coty.

"Old scars from a ship's propellor. Stay clear of
human ships like this one. I'm lucky I survived",
warns Mrs. Humpback.

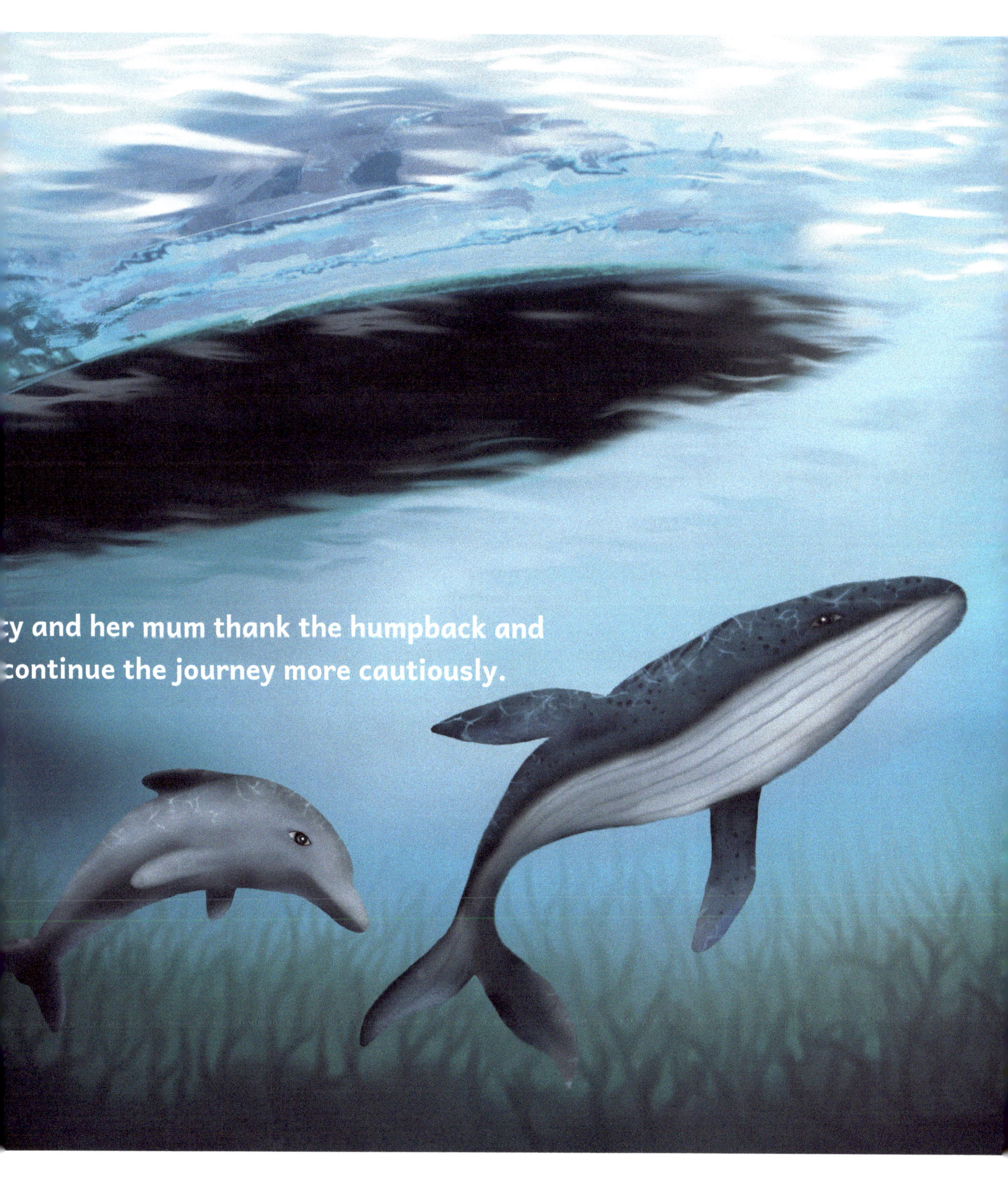

cy and her mum thank the humpback and
continue the journey more cautiously.

Having been swimming underwater for a while they
surface from time to time to breathe air.
As they reach the surface, to their dismay, they see a floating
island of plastic and rubbish.

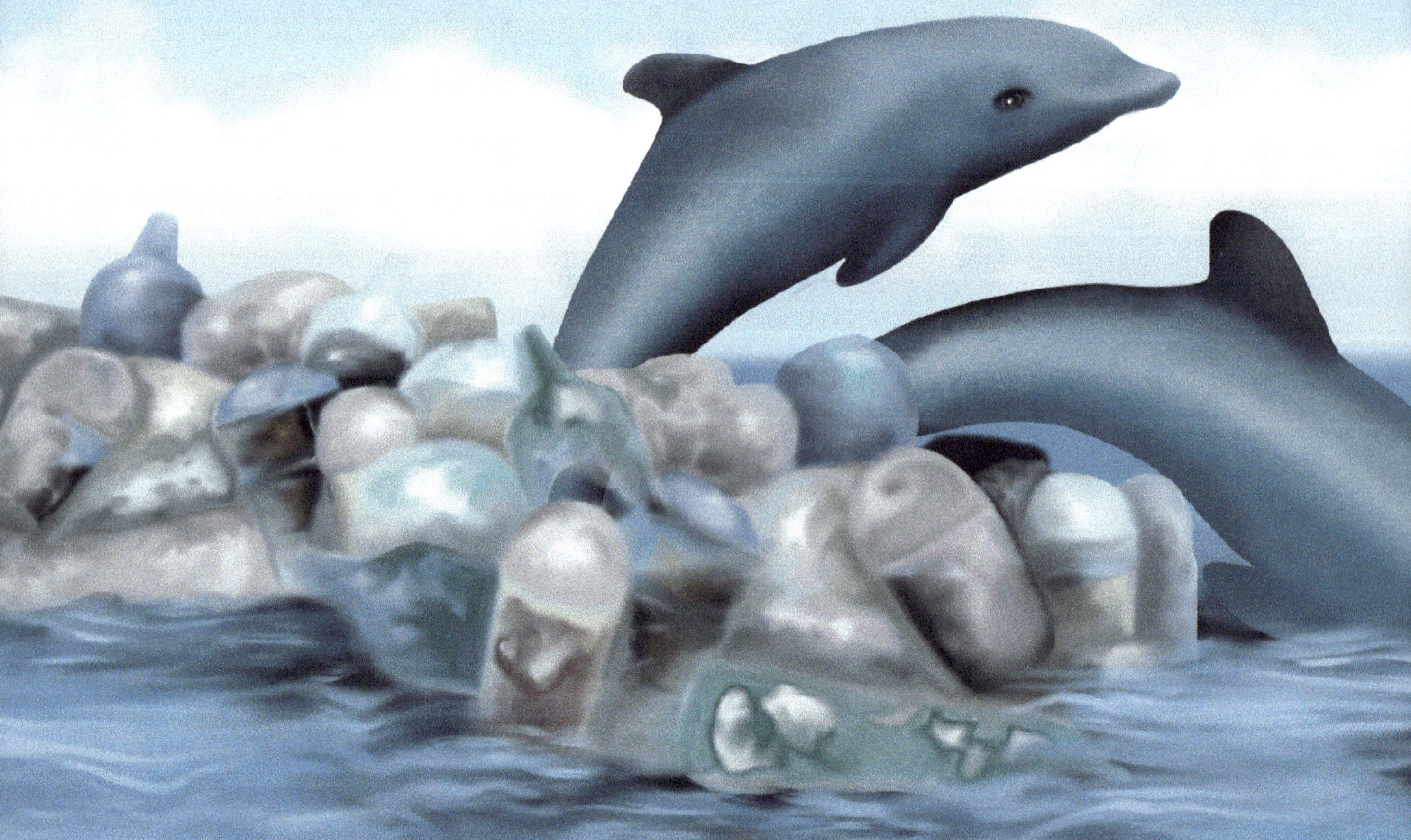

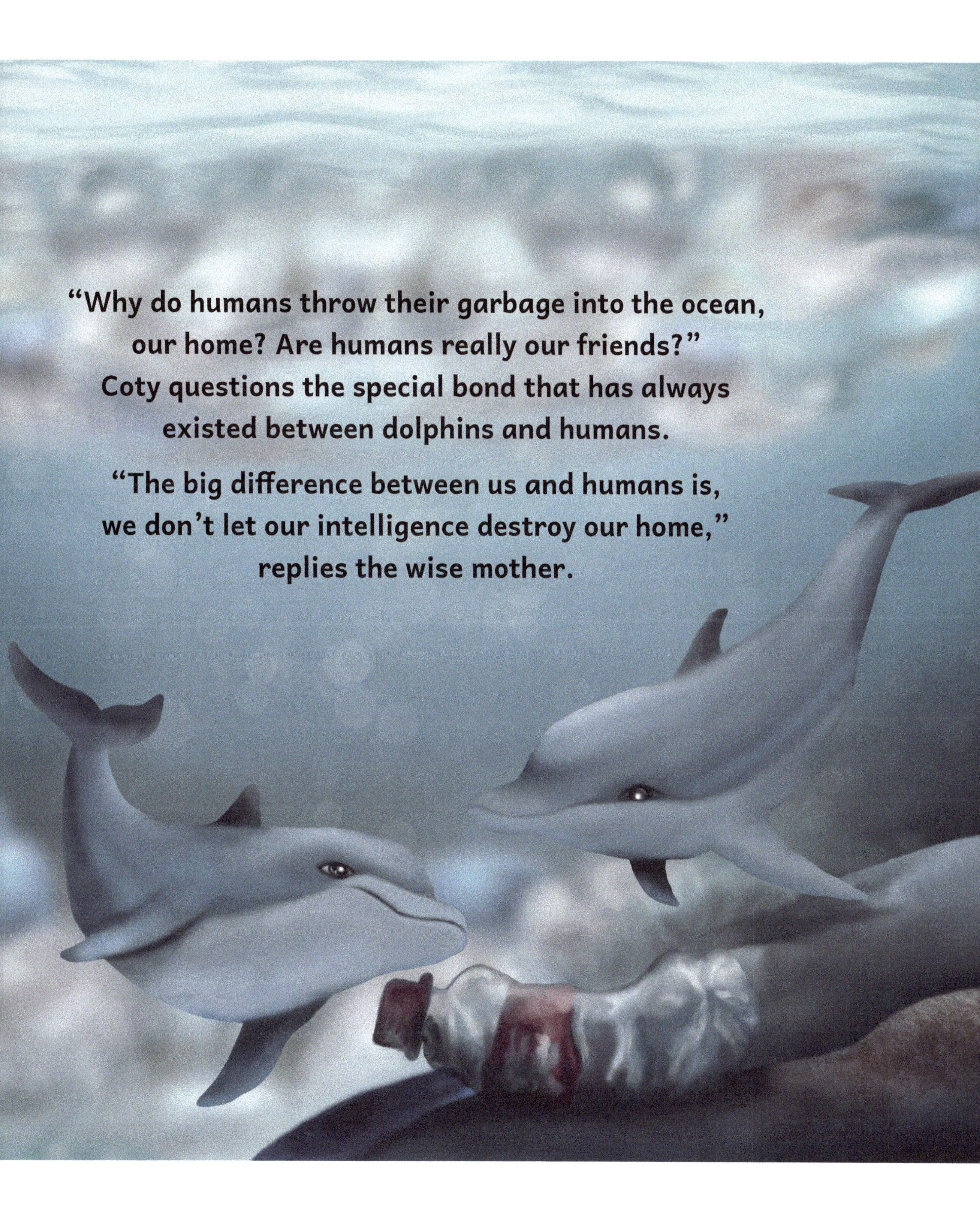
"Why do humans throw their garbage into the ocean,
our home? Are humans really our friends?"
Coty questions the special bond that has always
existed between dolphins and humans.

"The big difference between us and humans is,
we don't let our intelligence destroy our home,"
replies the wise mother.

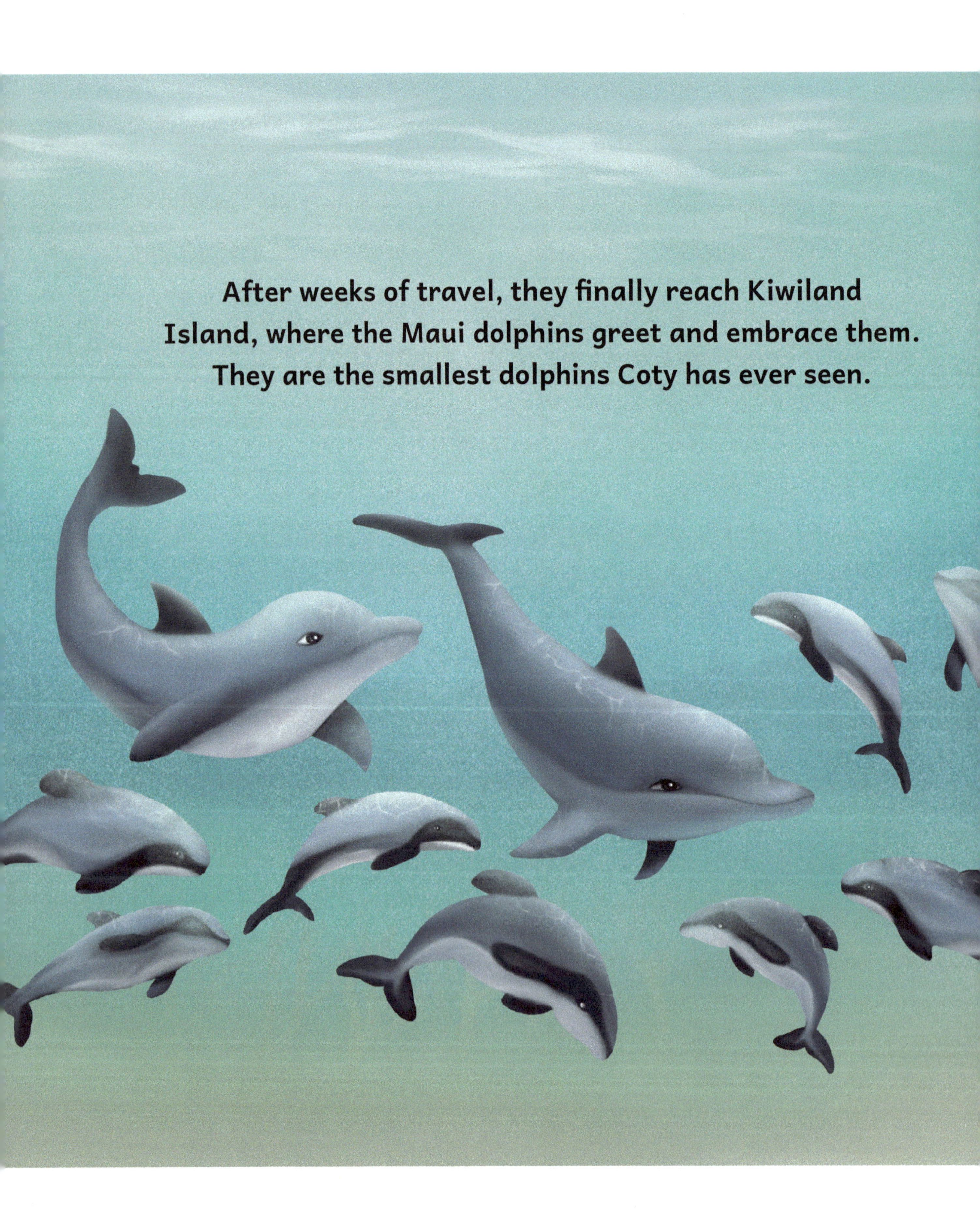

After weeks of travel, they finally reach Kiwiland
Island, where the Maui dolphins greet and embrace them.
They are the smallest dolphins Coty has ever seen.

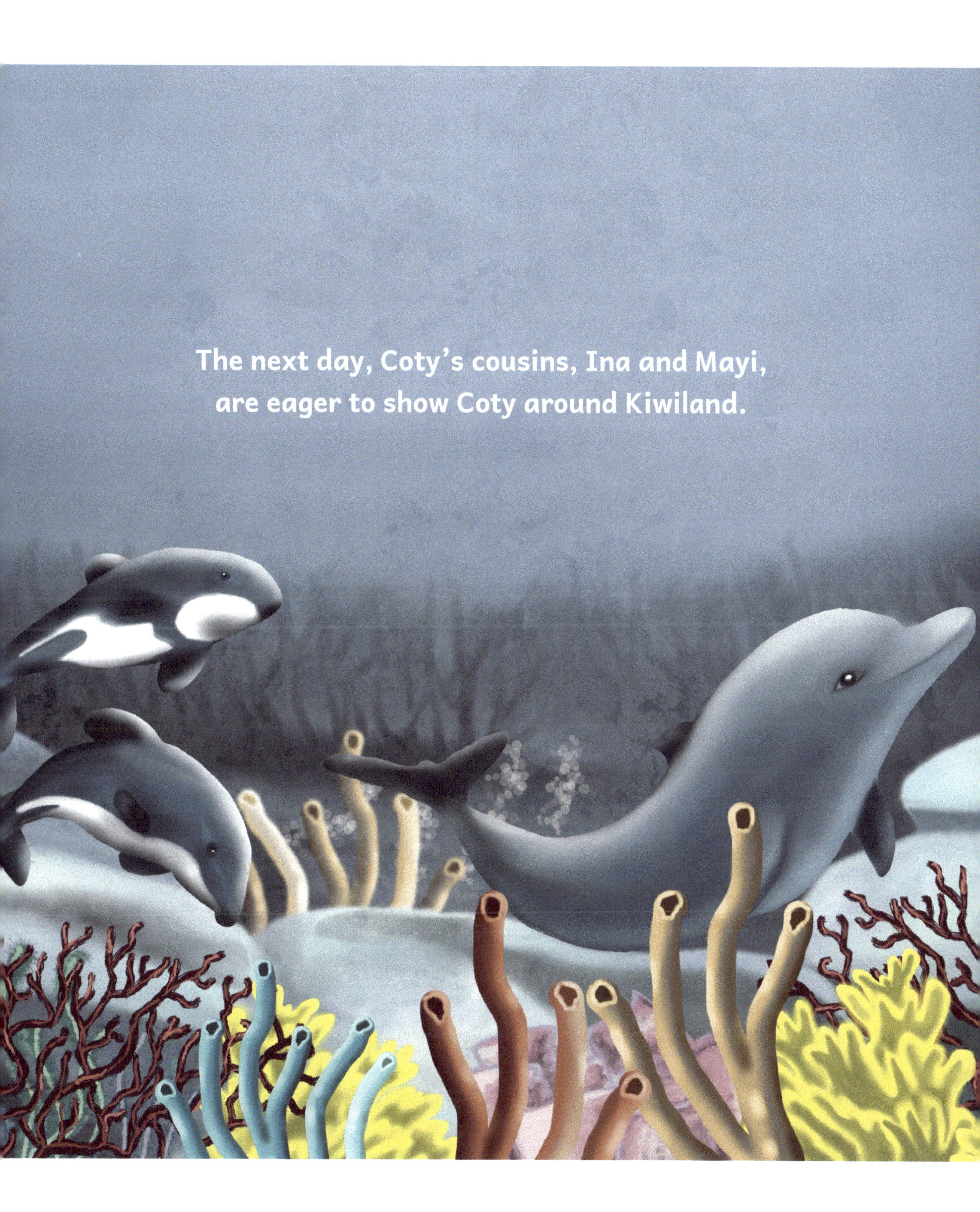
The next day, Coty's cousins, Ina and Mayi,
are eager to show Coty around Kiwiland.

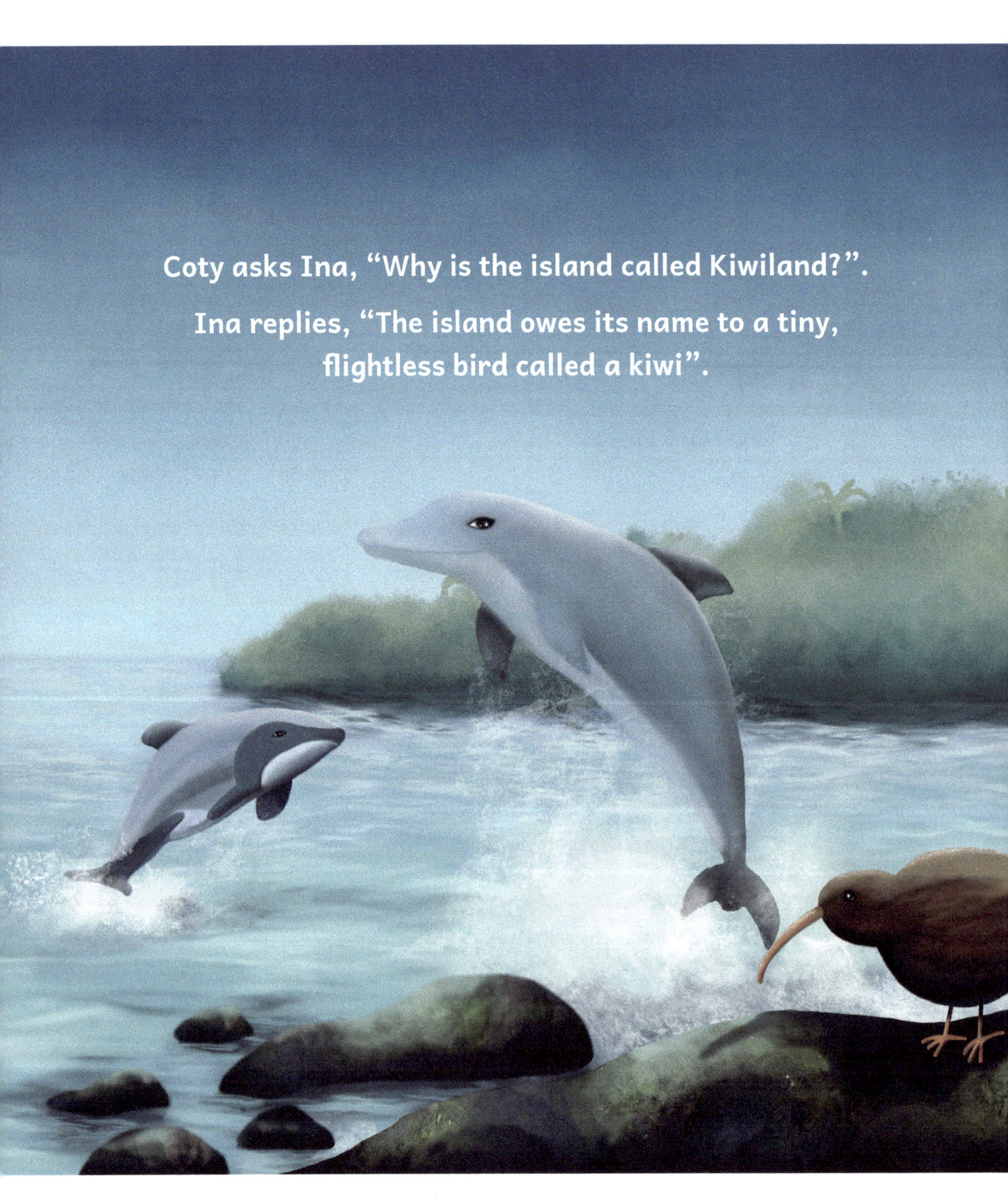
Coty asks Ina, "Why is the island called Kiwiland?".
Ina replies, "The island owes its name to a tiny,
flightless bird called a kiwi".

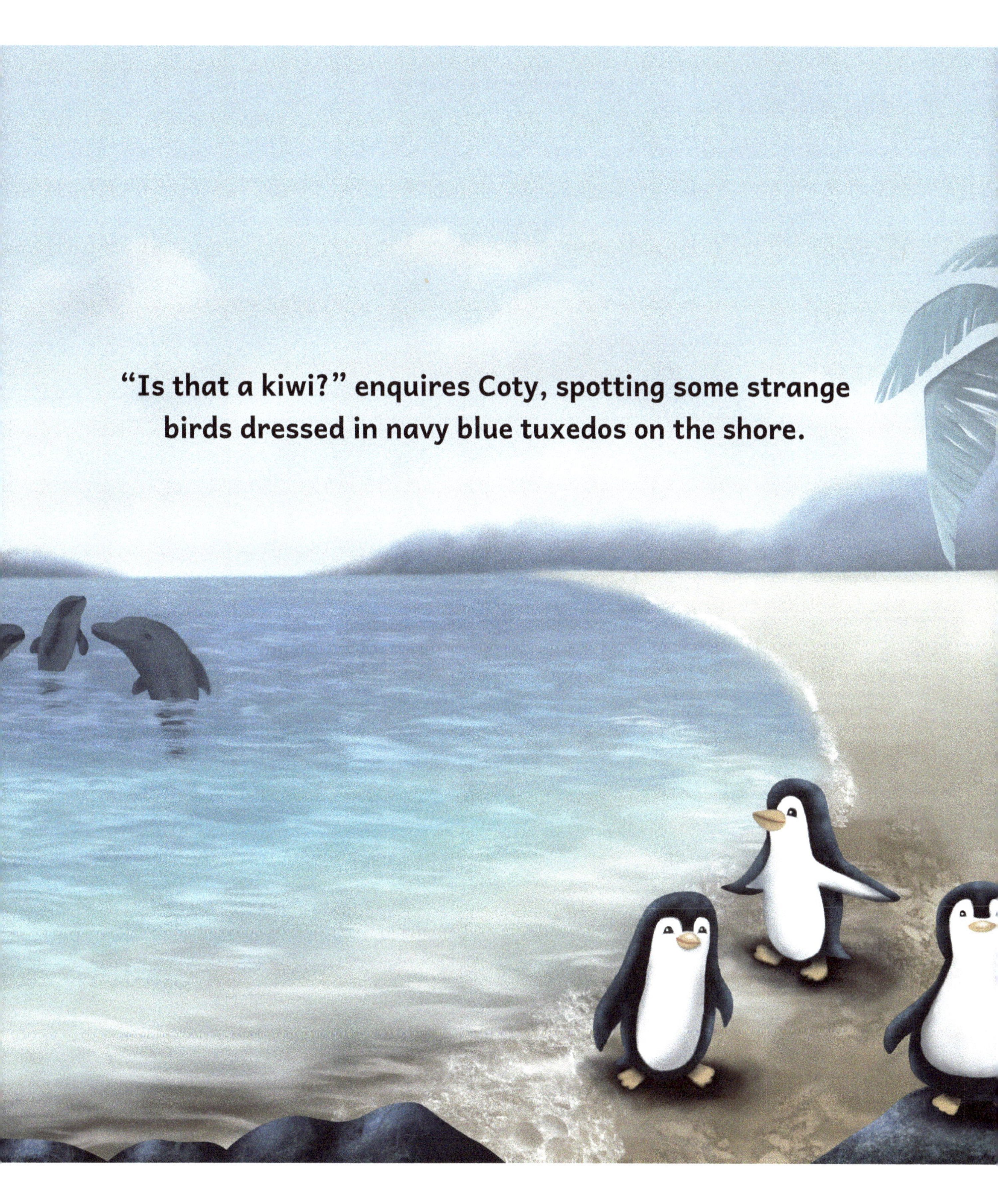
"Is that a kiwi?" enquires Coty, spotting some strange
birds dressed in navy blue tuxedos on the shore.

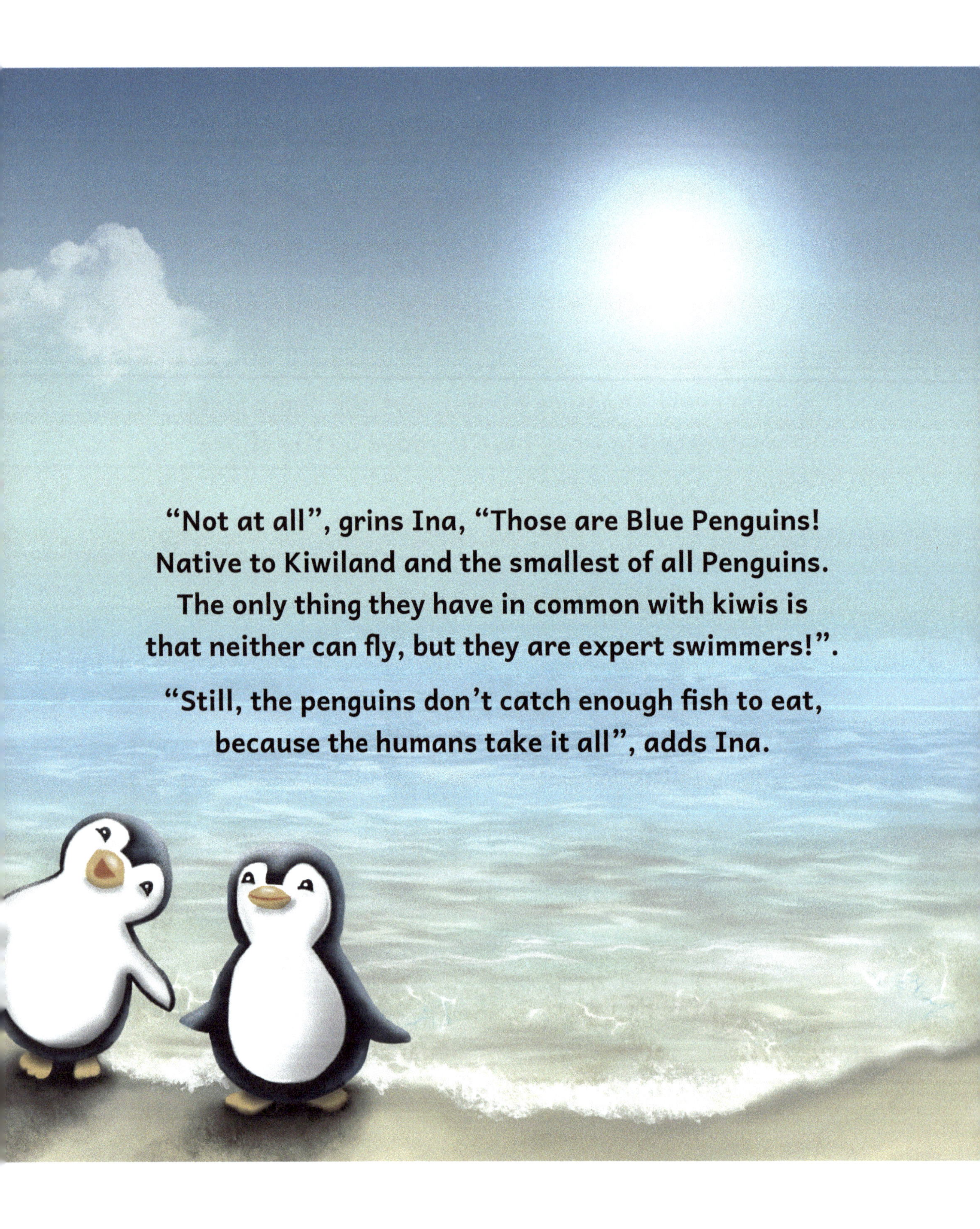

"Not at all", grins Ina, "Those are Blue Penguins!
Native to Kiwiland and the smallest of all Penguins.
The only thing they have in common with kiwis is
that neither can fly, but they are expert swimmers!".

"Still, the penguins don't catch enough fish to eat,
because the humans take it all", adds Ina.

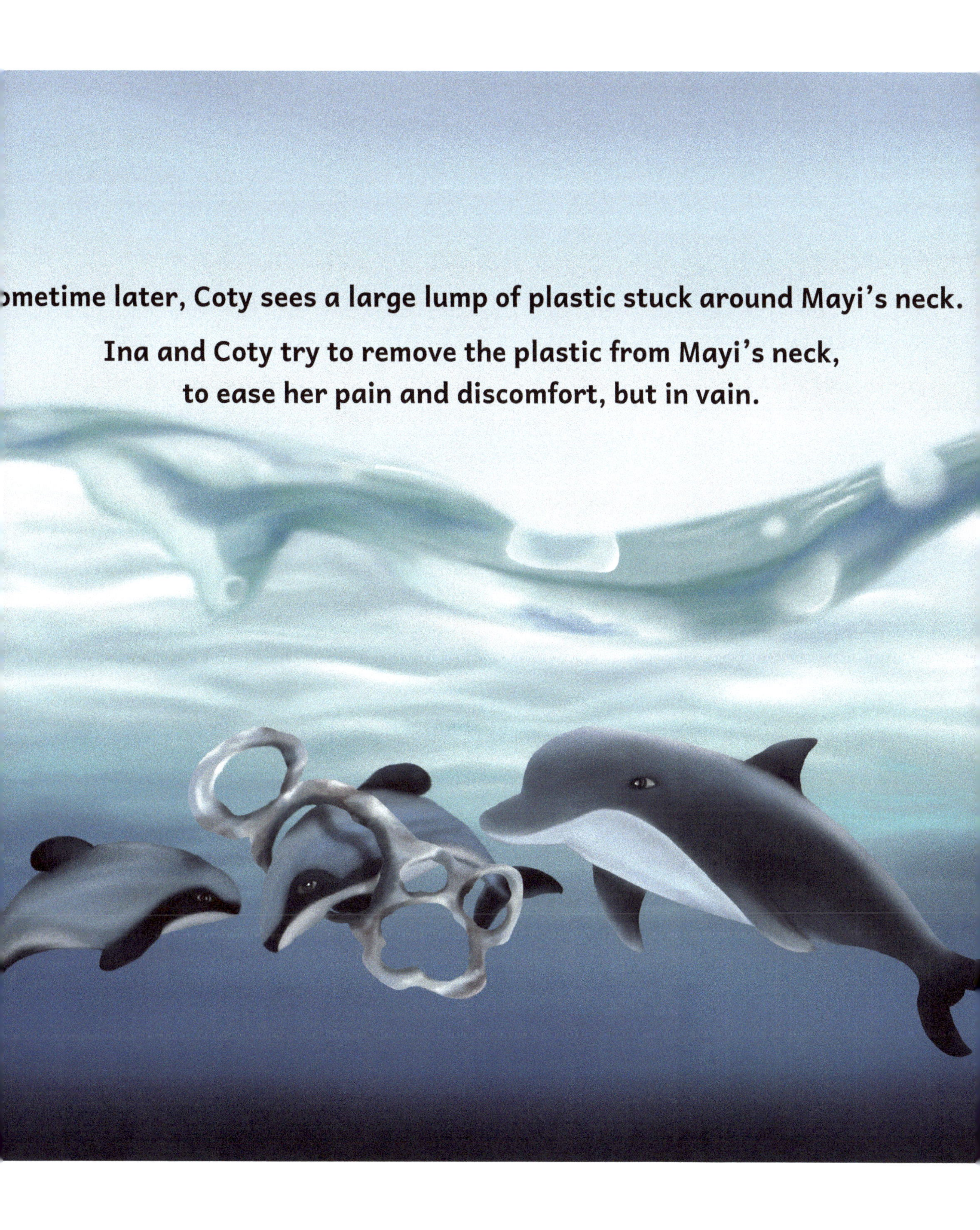
ometime later, Coty sees a large lump of plastic stuck around Mayi's neck.

Ina and Coty try to remove the plastic from Mayi's neck,
to ease her pain and discomfort, but in vain.

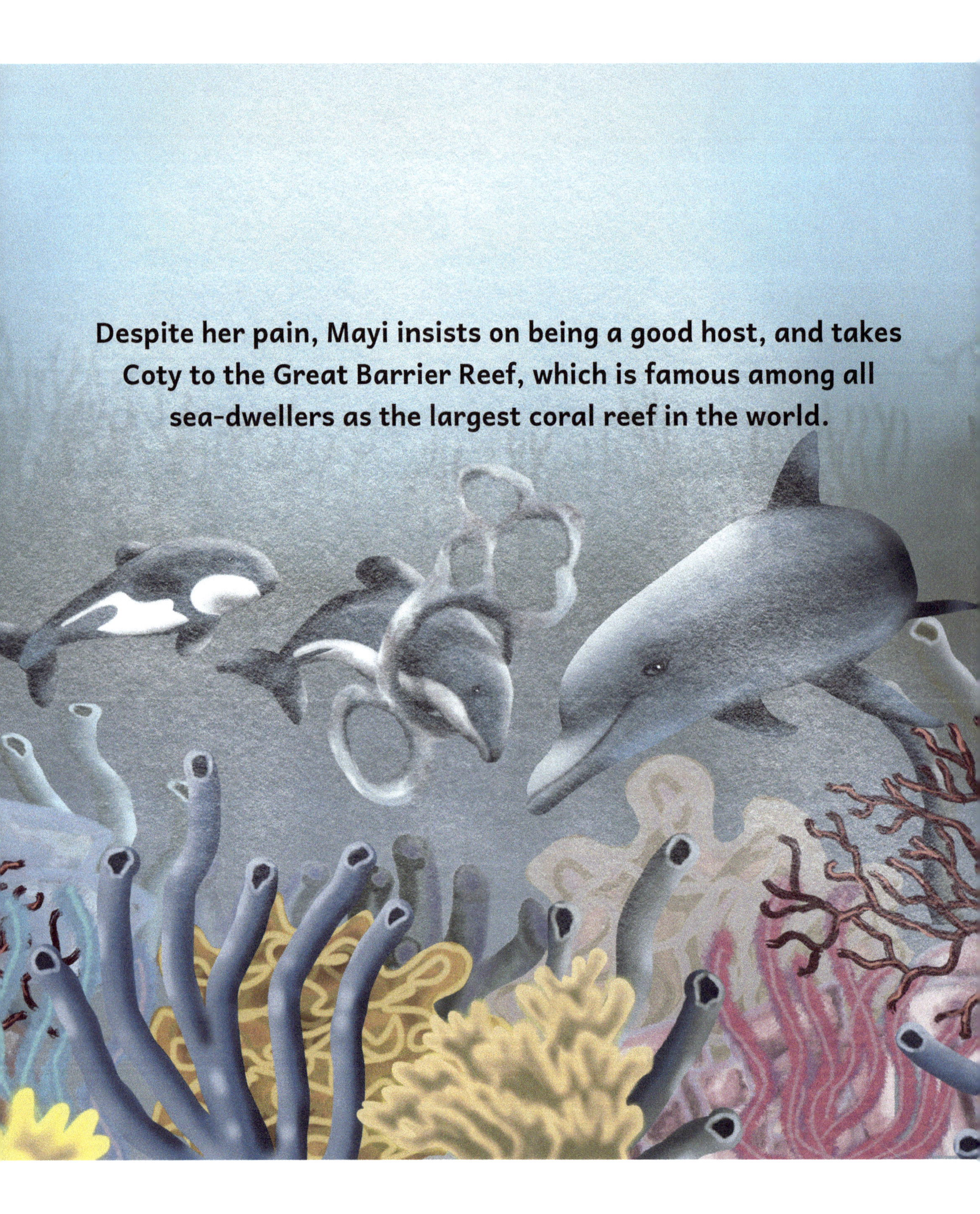
Despite her pain, Mayi insists on being a good host, and takes
Coty to the Great Barrier Reef, which is famous among all
sea-dwellers as the largest coral reef in the world.

When they arrive at the reef, Coty does not see the colourful reef she expects like the one back home on Nanao Island, but only corals that ave faded to skeletons of white. "Is this really the Great Barrier Reef? The most beautiful of all reefs?" she questions in disbelief.

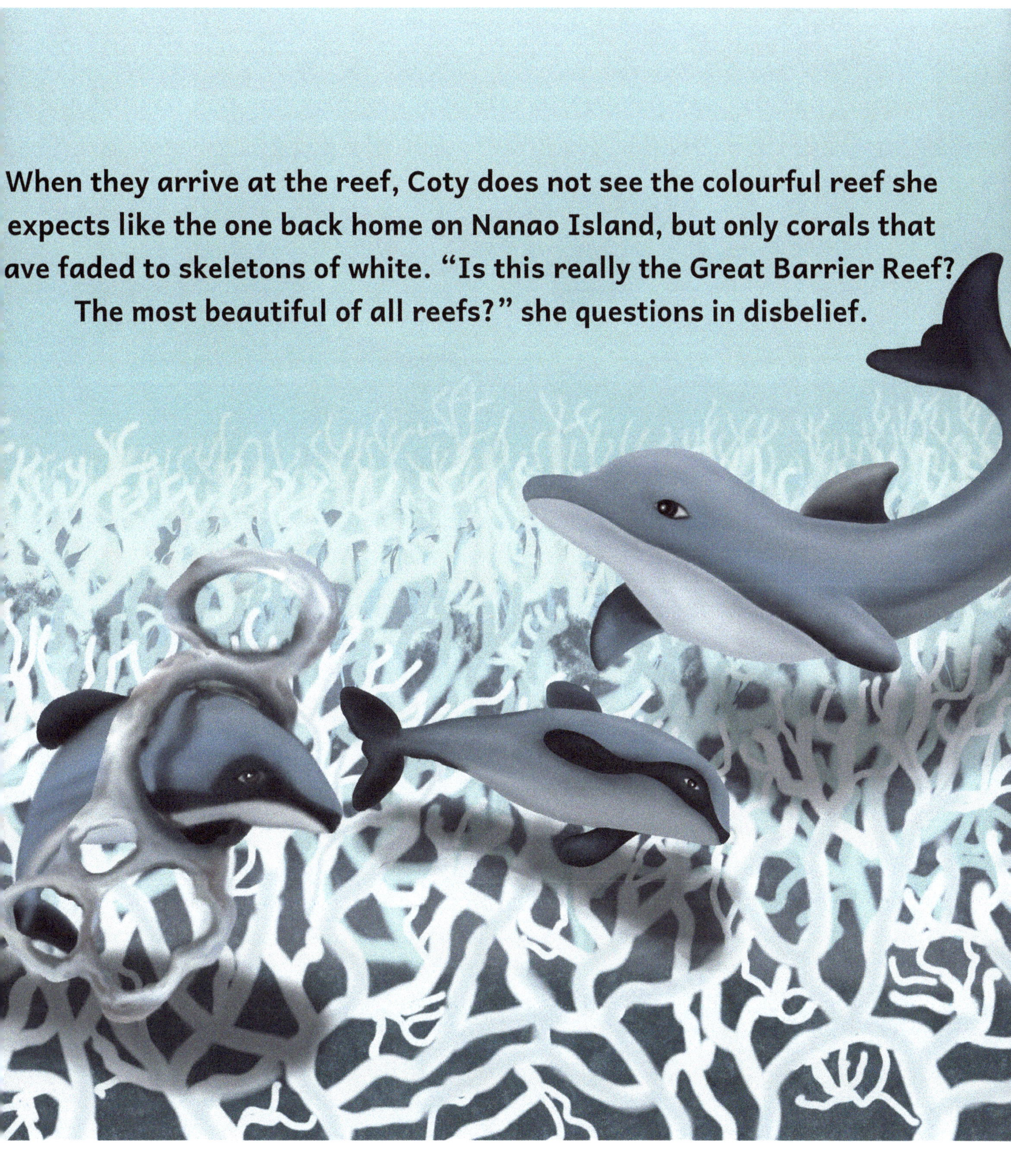

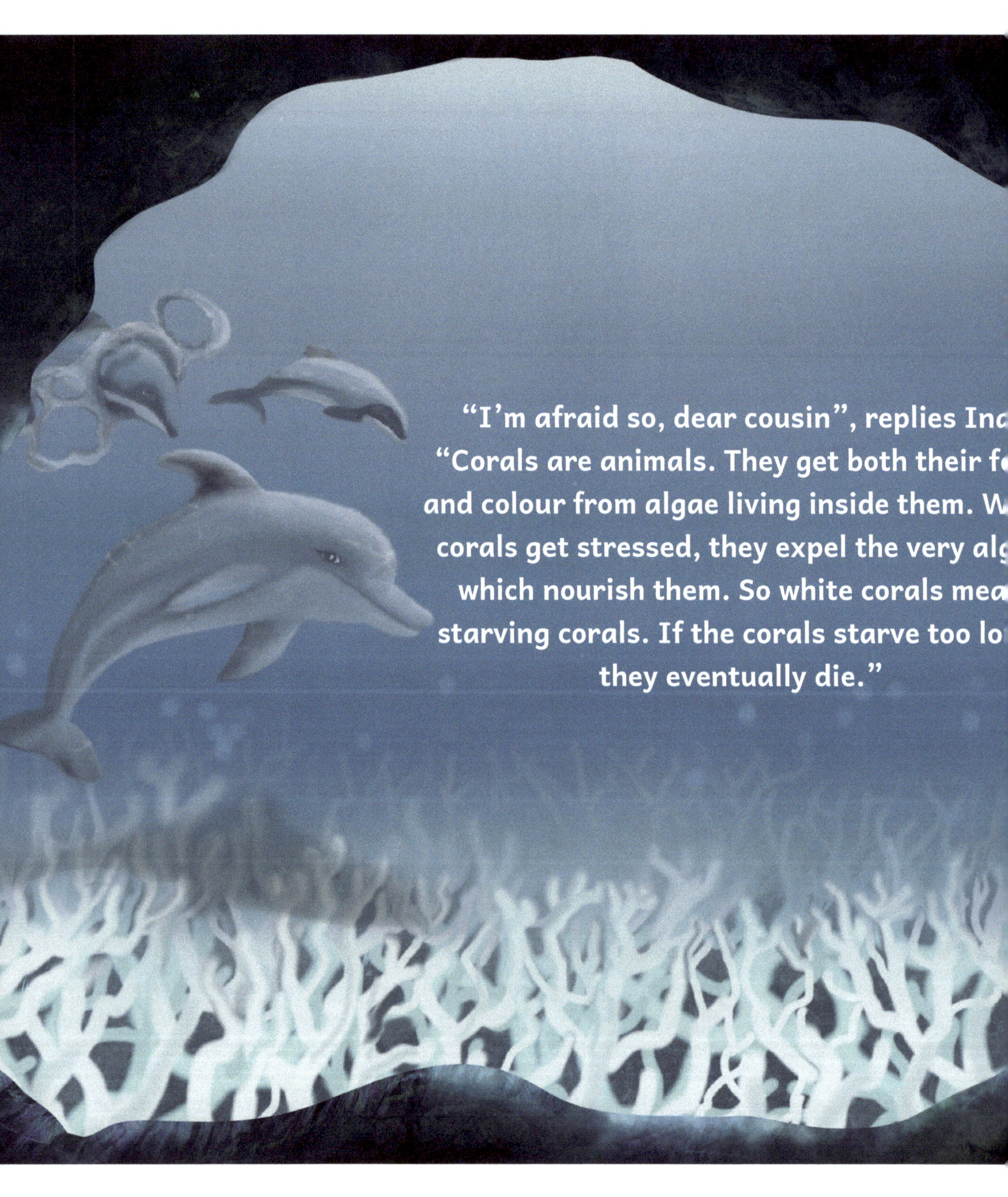
"I'm afraid so, dear cousin", replies Ind
"Corals are animals. They get both their f
and colour from algae living inside them. W
corals get stressed, they expel the very alg
which nourish them. So white corals mea
starving corals. If the corals starve too lo
they eventually die."

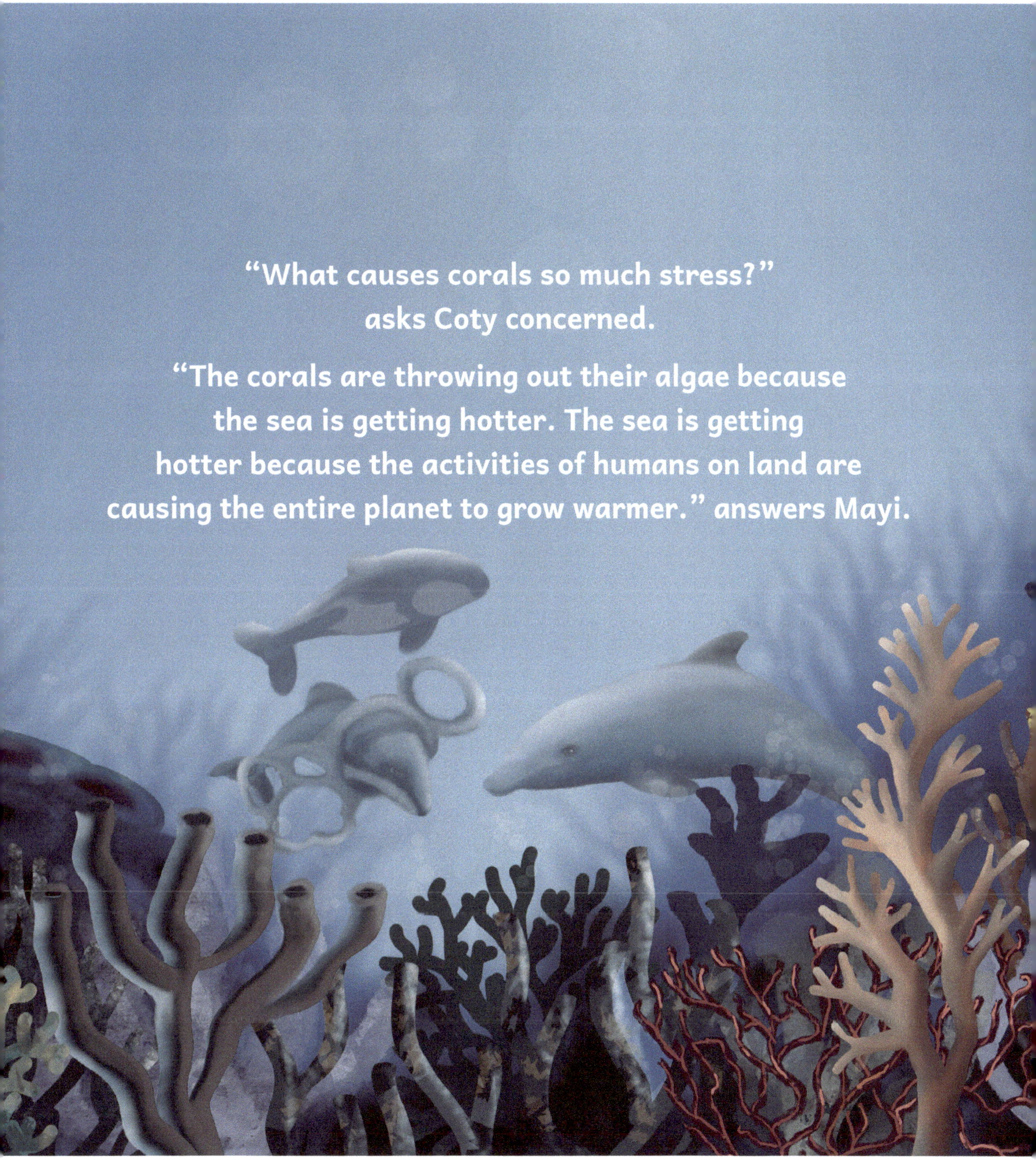

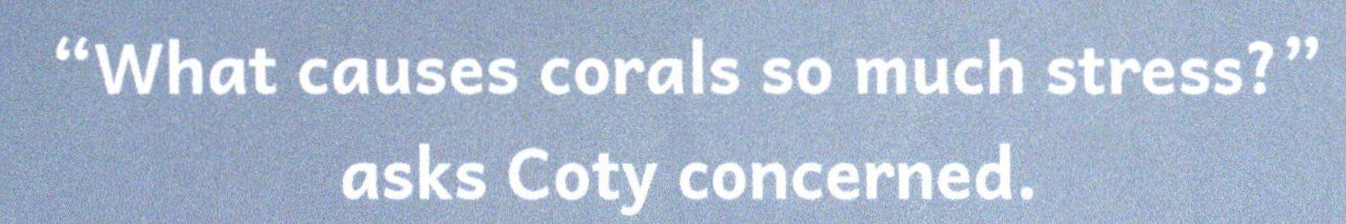

"What causes corals so much stress?"
asks Coty concerned.

"The corals are throwing out their algae because the sea is getting hotter. The sea is getting hotter because the activities of humans on land are causing the entire planet to grow warmer." answers Mayi.

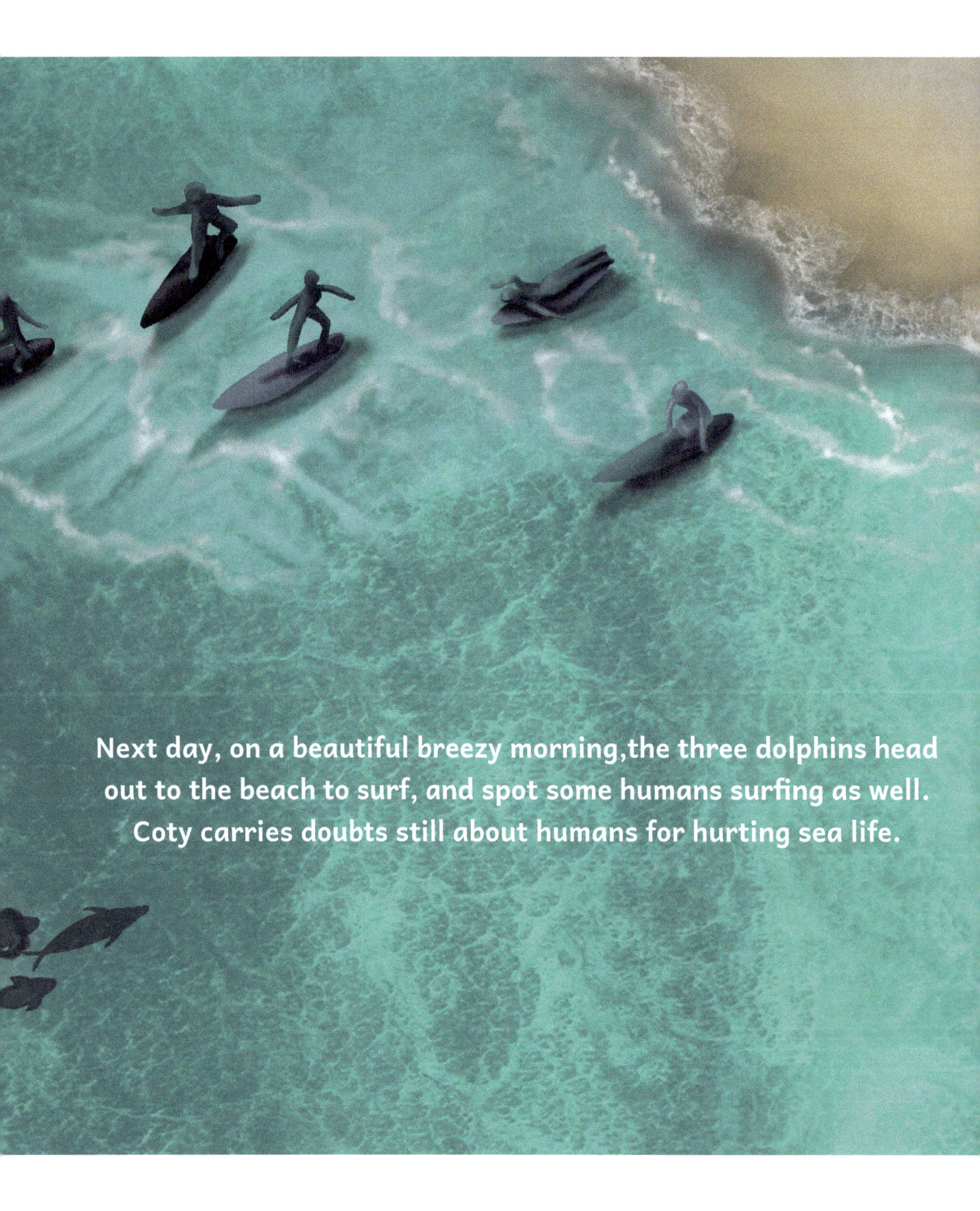

Next day, on a beautiful breezy morning,the three dolphins head out to the beach to surf, and spot some humans surfing as well. Coty carries doubts still about humans for hurting sea life.

Coty hesitates at first but seeing the waves cannot help join in the fun.
er all surfing is her favourite sport. A human mother and her small daughte
are also enjoying the surf close by.

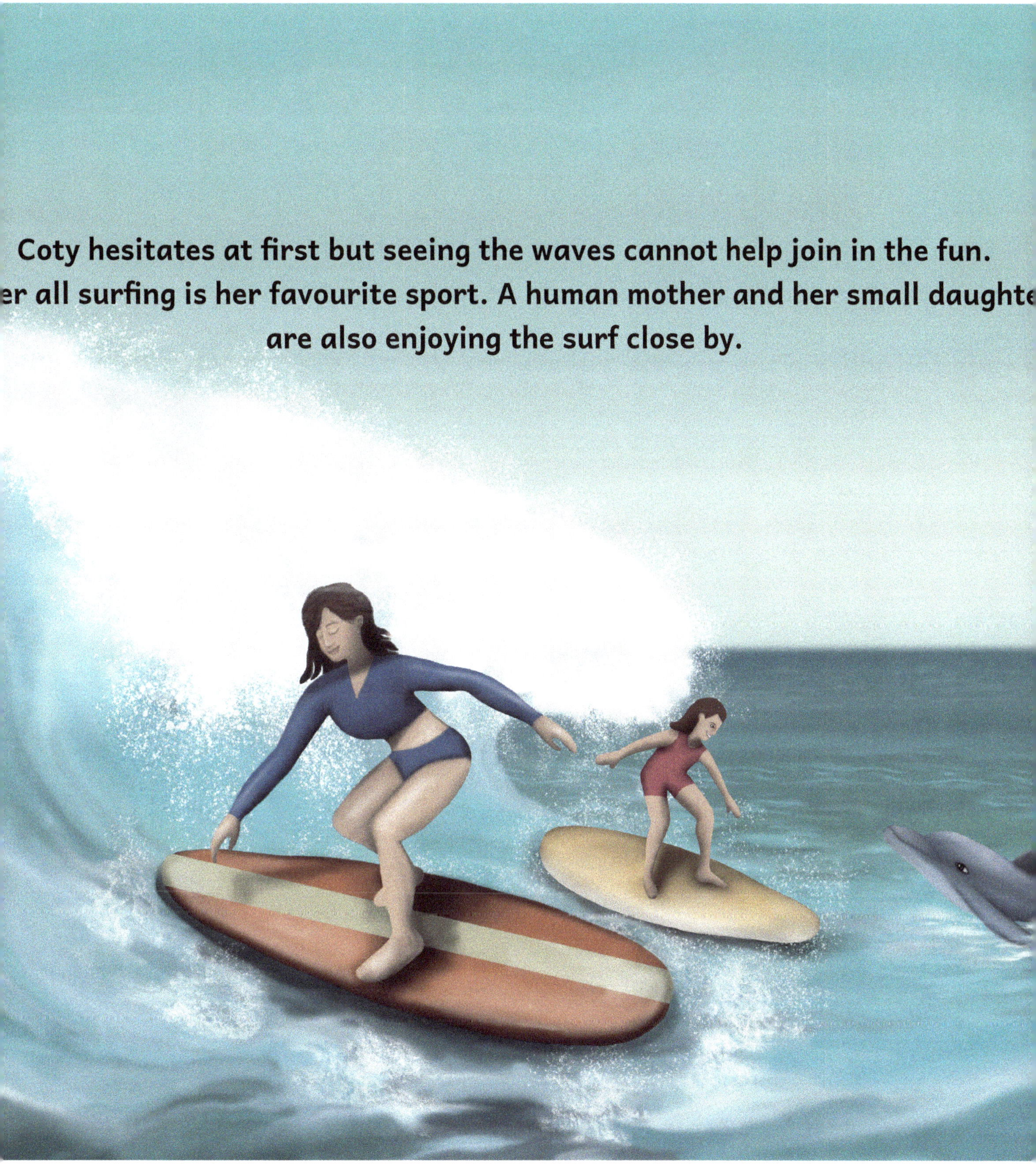

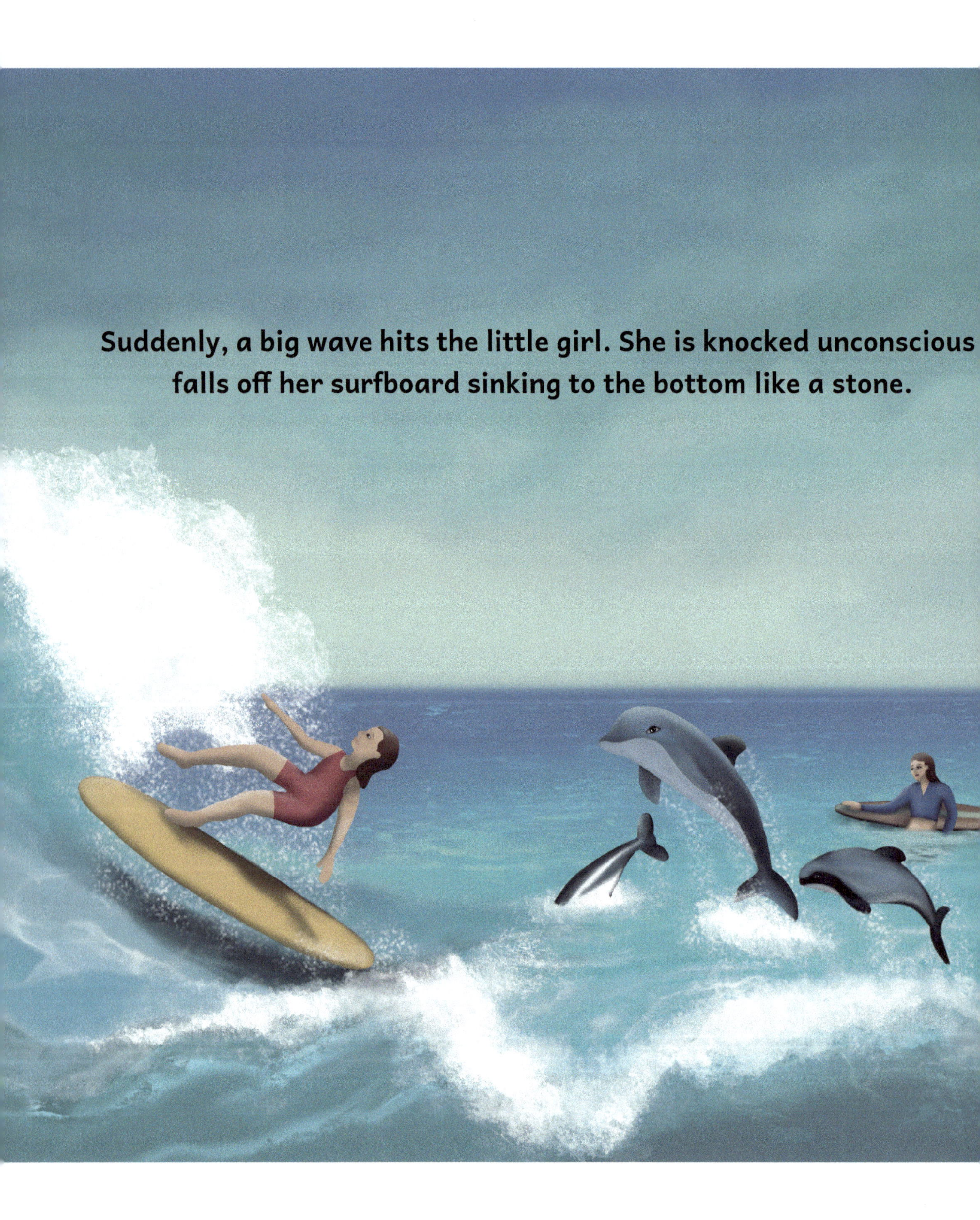
Suddenly, a big wave hits the little girl. She is knocked unconscious falls off her surfboard sinking to the bottom like a stone.

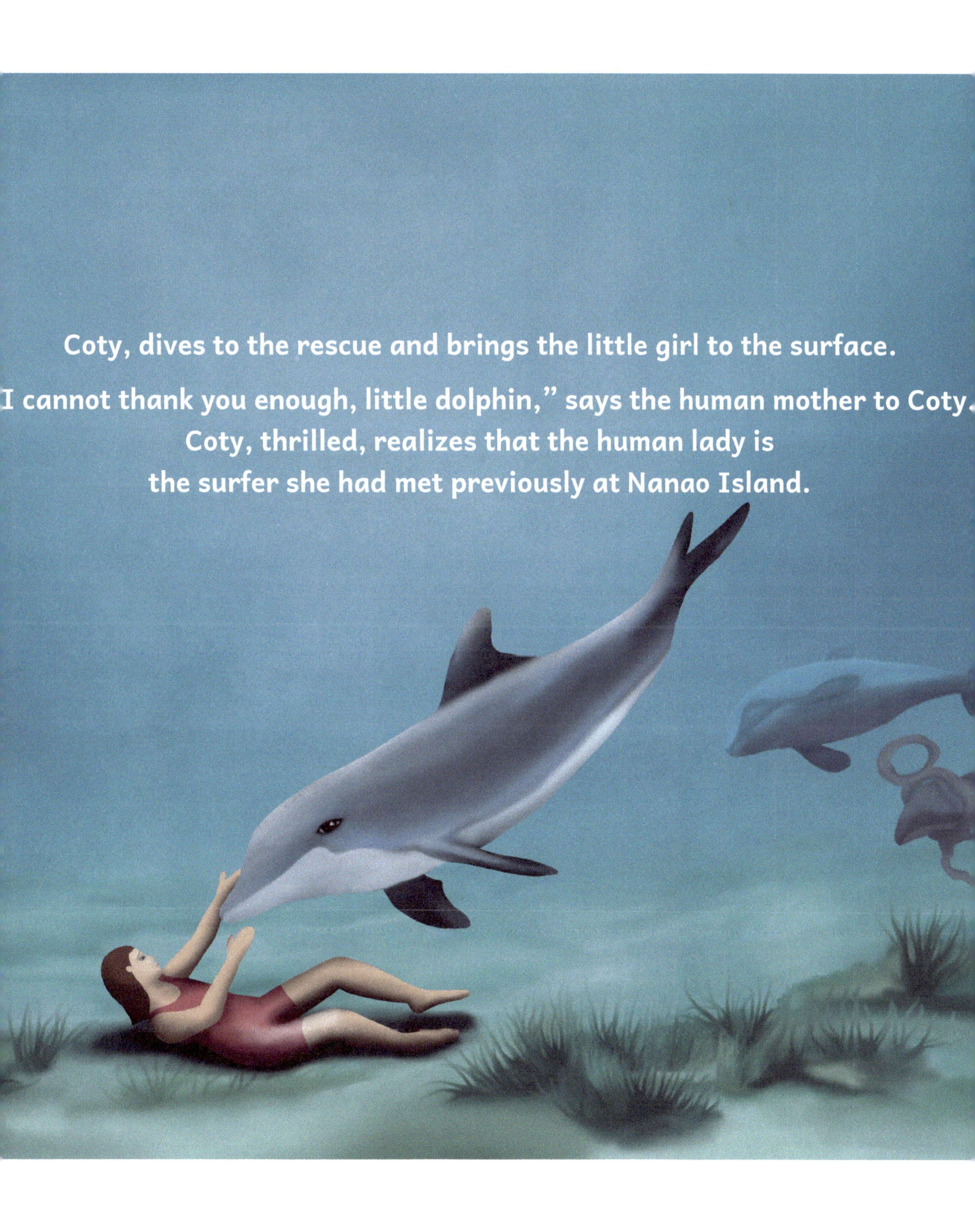
Coty, dives to the rescue and brings the little girl to the surface.
I cannot thank you enough, little dolphin," says the human mother to Coty.
Coty, thrilled, realizes that the human lady is
the surfer she had met previously at Nanao Island.

Coty invites the lady to meet Ina and Mayi. The lady notices the plastic entangled around Mayi's neck. "You poor thing!", she exclaims and removes the plastic gently, relieving Mayi from her agony at last.

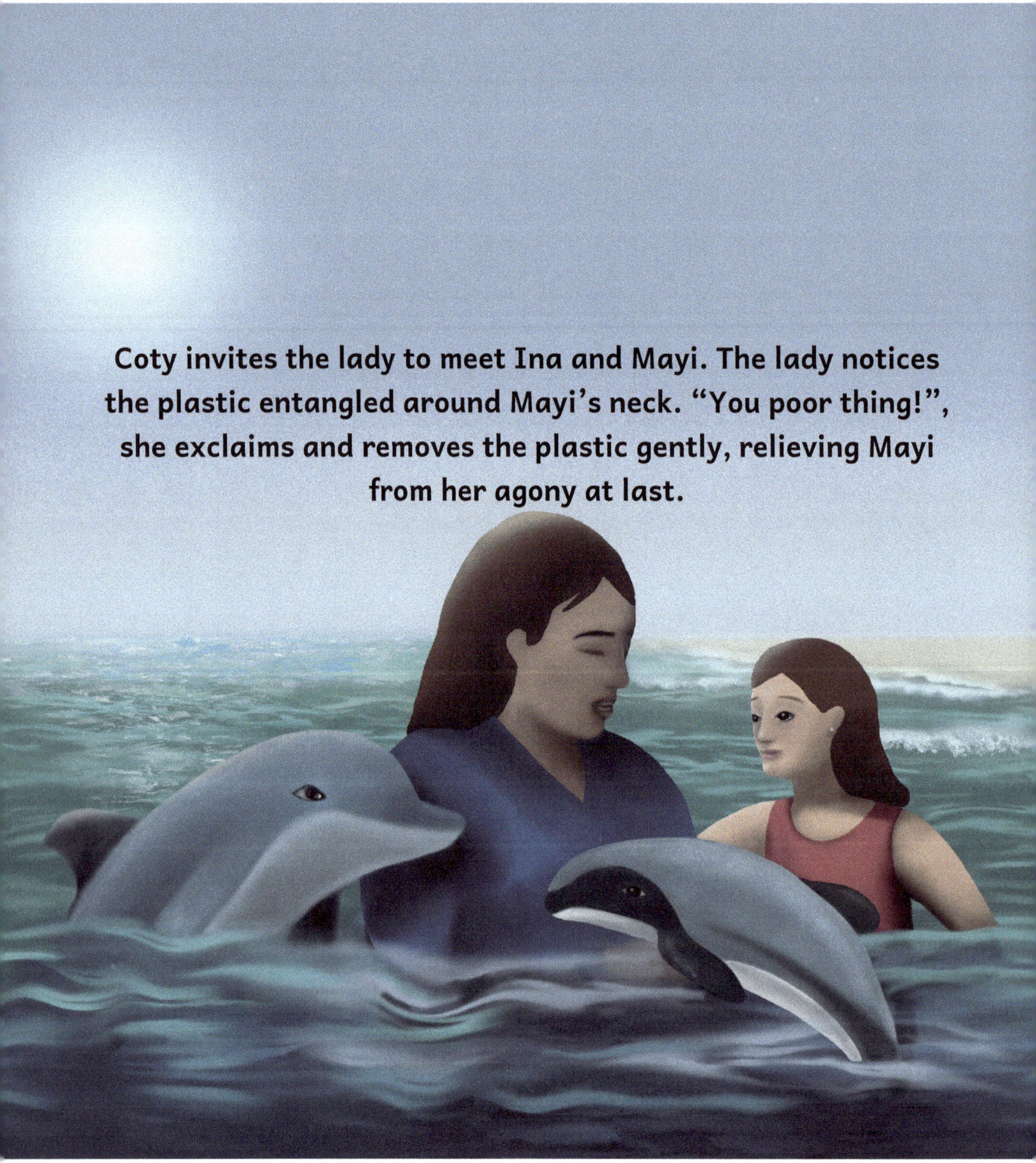

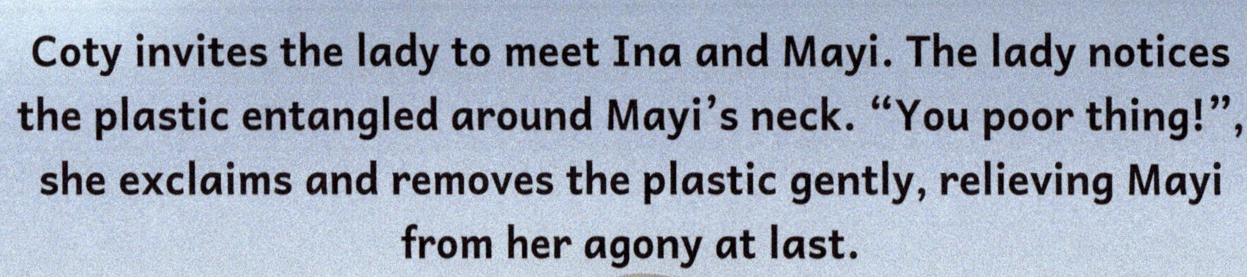

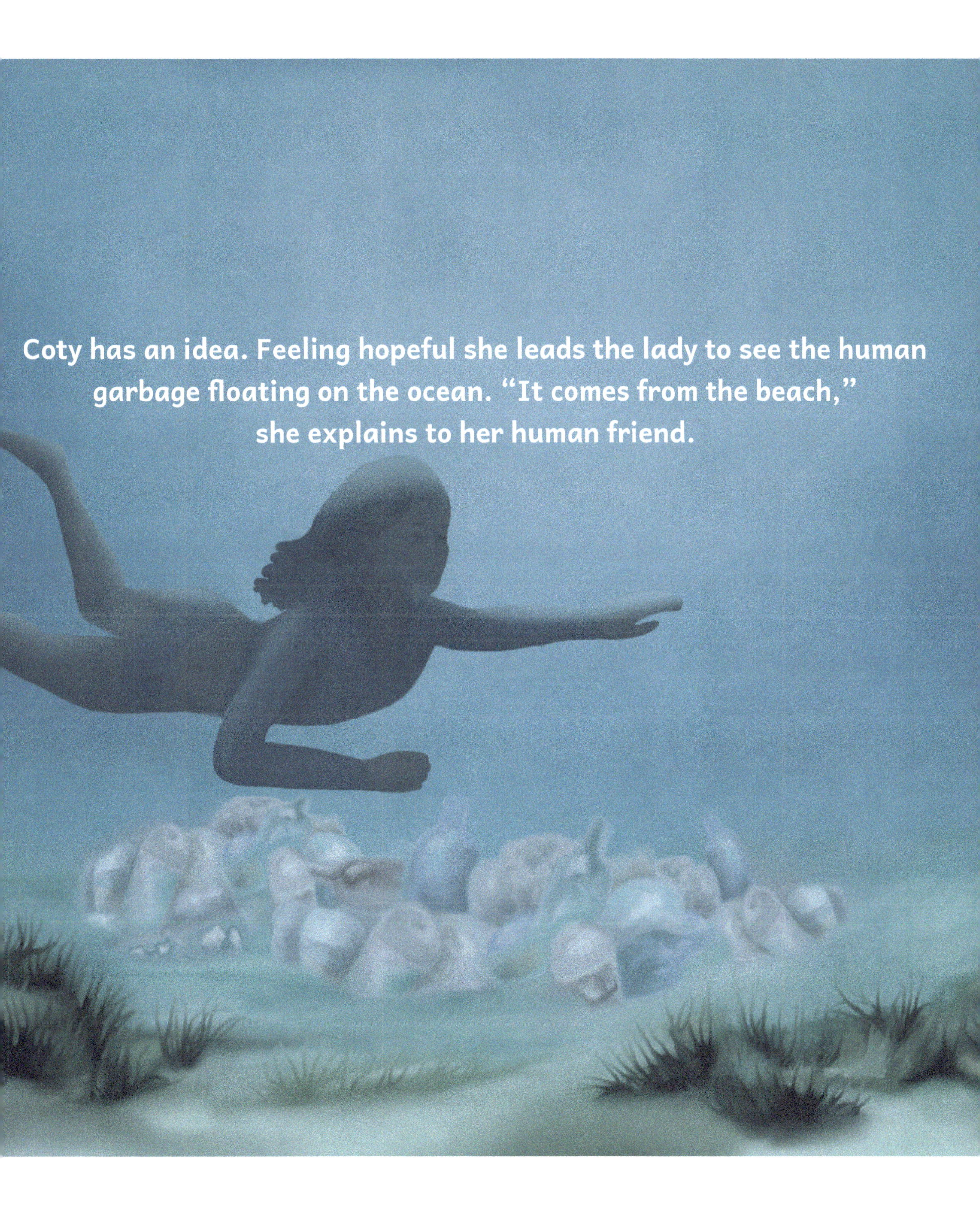

Coty has an idea. Feeling hopeful she leads the lady to see the human
garbage floating on the ocean. "It comes from the beach,"
she explains to her human friend.

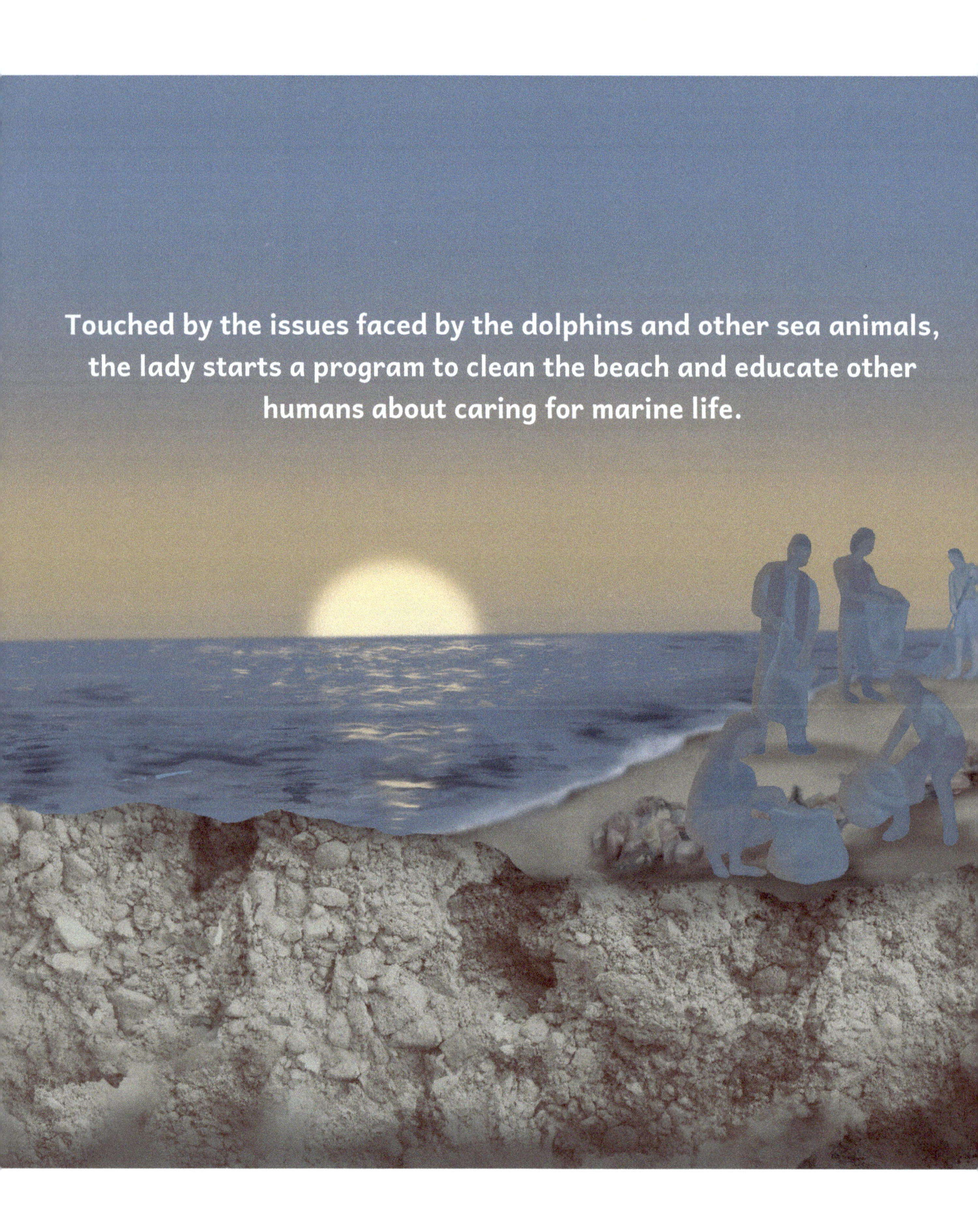
Touched by the issues faced by the dolphins and other sea animals, the lady starts a program to clean the beach and educate other humans about caring for marine life.

On her safe return to Kiwiland with her cousins,
Coty shares the adventure with her mother, "I still have hope.
Not all humans have ill intentions. I shall not stop believing in them."

THE END

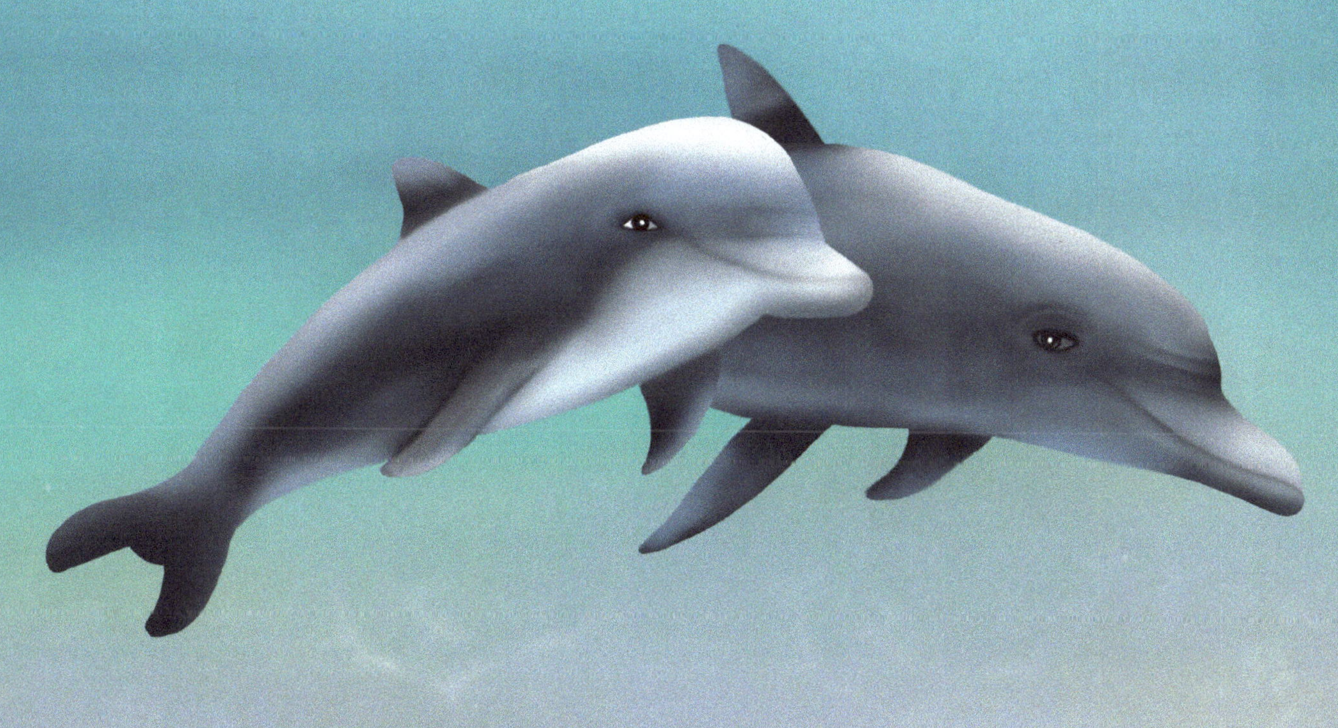

s:

at Barrier Reef is famous among all sea-dwellers as the largest coral reef i
tralia, close to New Zealand, where the imaginary Island, Kiwiland, is loca

phins make sounds called clicks to navigate underwater. Sound travels ove
ances in the form of waves at high speed. Surprisingly, under water sound
vel five times faster than in air.

guins have flippers for feet which make them expert swimmers.

phins have many things in common with the humans: they are mammals wh
birth, nurse their babies and nourish them with milk, are warm blooded an
ulate out body temperatures to remain warm even when it's cold outside.

ike fish, dolphins don't have gills, but lungs like the humans. Which means
e to periodically come up to the sea surface to breathe air.

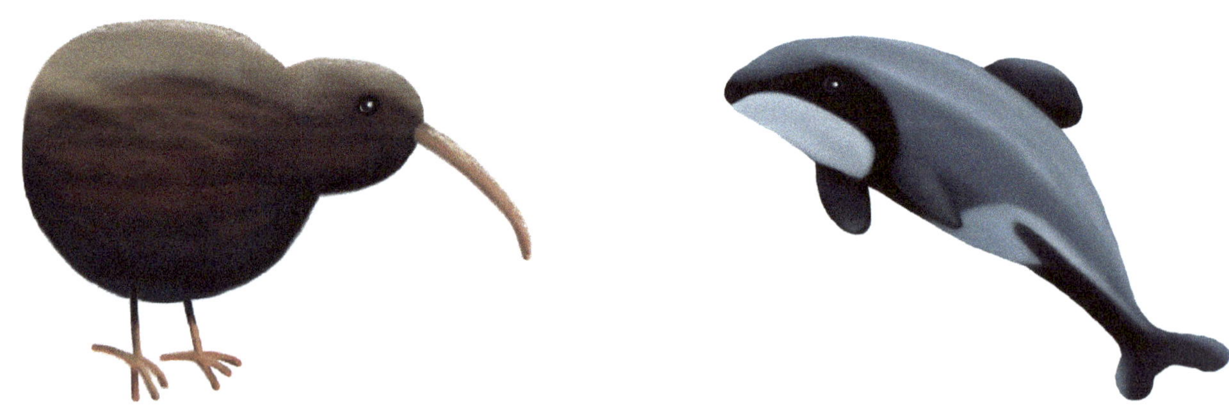